Christina —
Thanks for coming!
And the support.
D. Chesebro

Christina —
Enjoy! F#CK TRUMP!
Karen

ALTERNATIVE FACTS
An Adult Coloring Book

Welcome to our Alternative Facts. Or rather, our take on the bizarre turn of events in America since January 20, 2017. After all, we believe there can only ever be one set of facts — those based on the truth.

America is facing some serious issues as certain parties try to undermine the ideals and values that we hold dear. It seems like every day there is a new story that is disheartening, discouraging and sometimes devastating. But then we see events like the Women's March take place; we see average citizens standing up for their neighbors, no matter their race, religion or gender, and we see thousands forming activist groups or even running for office for the first time, and we are encouraged. Encouraged by and for the passion of American citizens for what is truly the American dream — life, liberty and the pursuit of happiness.

We hope you find these illustrations thought provoking, silly, and maybe even funny. But most of all, we hope you gather your friends, grab some crayons and your beverage of choice, and enjoy yourselves. Because although there is an important issue in need of your support — LGBTQ rights, women's reproductive rights, immigrant rights, environmental protection, removing dark money from our political process and holding our politicians accountable, to name a few — this is going to be a long four years and we all need a good laugh occasionally.

Proceeds from the sale of this coloring book will be donated to charities and non-profits that have been affected by current events and to those organizations that continue to fight to keep our constitutional freedoms intact. Please visit our Facebook and Instagram accounts at **@AlternativeFactsColoringBook** or email us at **alternativefactscoloringbook@gmail.com** for more details.

Happy coloring!

Illustrator's Note

When I was approached to do this project in March, I couldn't have imagined — I don't think anyone could have imagined — things going down the way they did. Over the course of little more than half a year, as the political climate darkened and my anxiety turned into fear and depression (after all, I check many of the boxes this administration seems bent on hating: child of immigrants, person of color, not entirely straight, etc. ...), this project became a source of comfort for me. As an artist, I know how creation can be a form of subversion, and in a time of what seems like unending destruction and oppression, this project has become my personal resistance, my way of keeping sane given the current political climate, while protesting the administration and raising money for a good cause with the skills that I have.

Though I have poured many long hours into this project, I am not under any delusions that this simple coloring book will solve America's deepest systemic inequalities or bring world peace. That would be a very nice thought, but the truth is, we didn't even manage to cover all of the many, many wrongdoings this administration has been involved in or endorsed, either outright or tacitly. And we know that by the time this gets to you, there will be illustrations that are incorrect or no longer relevant, and probably enough material to fill a whole second volume. Regardless, I hope that you enjoy this coloring book, and that you will be inspired to find your own resistance through creation, whether it is through drawing, writing letters, organizing movements, fundraising, etc. At the very least, I hope that by grabbing your art tools of choice and sitting down for a few hours, these dark times can seem a little brighter and more colorful. I'd like to give a special thanks to all my friends and family who have supported me in the making of this project, and to you, anonymous colorist, for supporting us and helping a good cause!

53% of men, 42% of women, 58% of white voters, 8% of black voters and 29% of Latino voters elected Donald Trump, according to the Pew Research Center.

On January 21, 2017, Donald Trump started his presidency with White House Press Secretary Sean Spicer falsely claiming that the crowd on the National Mall was the **"largest audience to ever witness an inauguration."**

As of September 8, 2017, Trump has told **1,145 lies**, according to the *Washington Post*'s interactive database.

On January 21, 2017, an estimated **725,000 people** converged on Washington, D.C. and an estimated **4.1 million people** marched and protested throughout the world. Linda Sarsour, Tamika Mallory, Carmen Perez, and Vanessa Wruble organized the Women's March on Washington. It is the **largest single-day protest in U.S. history**.

Check out the estimates on crowd attendance by Jeremy Pressman, a professor of political science at the University of Connecticut, and Erica Chenoweth, a professor at the University of Denver and an expert on nonviolent protest, here:
https://goo.gl/u6jWeP

President Trump proclaims April 2017 as National Sexual Assault Awareness Month.

"Women, you have to treat them like shit."
— Donald Trump, *New York Magazine*, 1992

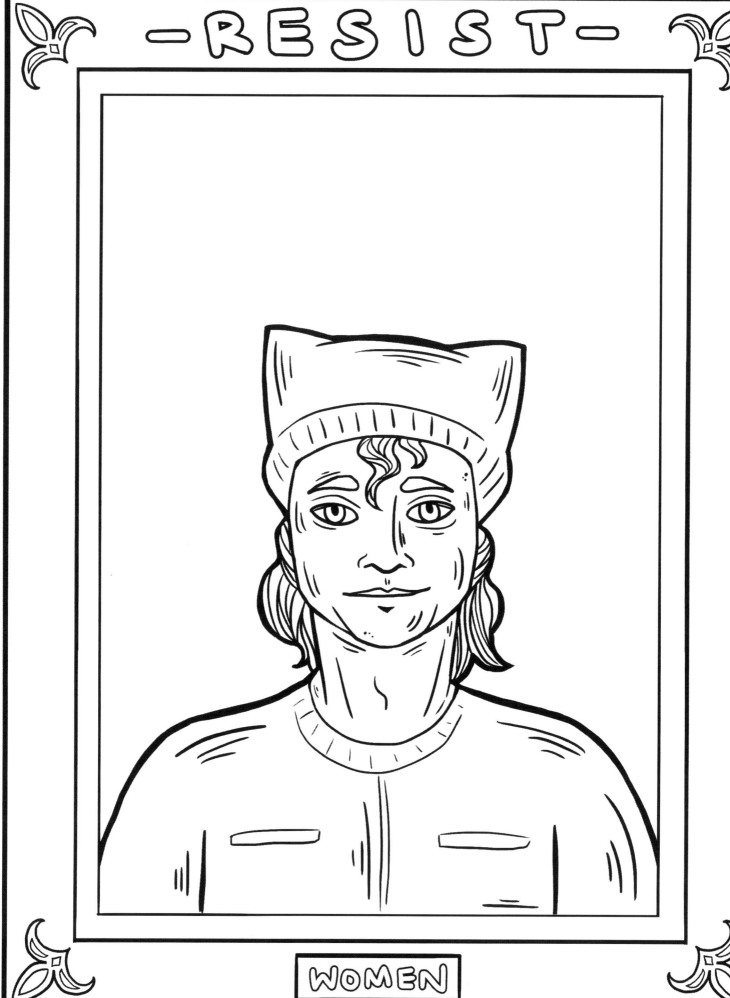

The **Pussyhat Project** was started in anticipation of the Women's March in Washington, D.C.

Visit their website to learn more about their work, find patterns to make your own hat, and discover ways to be involved: **www.pussyhatproject.com**

30 protesters braved the cold in **Paradise Bay, Antarctica** to join the global Women's March.

On January 20, 2017, after the **National Parks Service's official Twitter account (@NatlParkService)** tweeted images unfavorably comparing President Trump's inauguration to President Obama's, the US Department of Interior was ordered to freeze it's official social media account.

On January 24, 2017, the **Badlands National Park's Twitter account (@BadlandsNPS)** tweeted a series of facts about climate change after the Trump administration barred the Environmental Protection Agency from sharing news releases, blog updates or posts on its social media accounts. **Trump has publicly stated that climate change is a "hoax."**

While those tweets were eventually deleted, unofficial accounts, such as **@AltNatParkSer** and **@BadHombreNPS**, were quickly set up and continue to tweet.

TRUMP is FAKE NEWS

NOT MY CHEETO

YOU'VE FUCKED UP... #BIGLY

Senator Bernie Sanders (D-VT) was one of two leading candidates to campaign for the Democratic presidential nomination, but lost the nomination to Hillary Clinton.

Hillary Clinton was the official Democratic presidential candidate, winning the nomination over Bernie Sanders (D-VT). Although she **won the national popular vote** in the general election, she **lost the electoral vote.**

According to David Wasserman of the nonpartisan Cook Political Report, Clinton won the popular vote with 65.8 million votes while Trump took 62.9 million votes. Check the statistics of the popular vote here: **https://goo.gl/u9Ax9G**

After acting as Trump's campaign CEO, **Stephen Bannon**, the former chief executive of *Breitbart News*, was selected by Trump as his Chief Strategist (a special position created just for Bannon) and senior Counselor. Reports from the White House say **many of the executive orders issued by Trump were crafted by Bannon and Stephen Miller.**

Bannon left the White House on **August 18, 2017**.

Donald John Trump
45th President of the United States

Great Seal of the United States

Addison Mitchell "Mitch" McConnell Jr.
Republican Senator from Kentucky; Majority Leader of the Senate

The CIA reported that Russia hacked the servers of both the Republican National Convention and the Democratic National Convention. Wikileaks has released close to 20,000 e-mails from the DNC leak, while roughly 200 e-mails from the RNC have been released elsewhere online.

"It is the assessment of the intelligence community that Russia's goal here was to favor one candidate over the other, to help Trump get elected. That's the consensus view."
— An unnamed senior intelligence official

Senator Mitch McConnell has dismissed the veracity of the intelligence communities' reports and rebuffed efforts to build a select committee to investigate further.

Shortly after the election, McConnell's wife, **Elaine Chao**, was nominated for **Secretary of Transportation**. She assumed office on **January 31, 2017**.

On August 9, 2017, Trump and McConnell were reported by the *New York Times* to have engaged in a shouting match during a phone call. It is reported that Trump was angry at McConnell's refusal to protect him from the investigation into the Russian election interference.

Seal of the Commonwealth of Kentucky

Jared Corey Kushner
Senior Advisor to the President, Trump's son-in-law

Rex Wayne Tillerson
69th United States Secretary of State and ExxonMobil's chairman and chief executive officer of the company from 2006 to 2016

Vladimir Vladimirovich Putin
President of Russia

Russian Coat of Arms

A set of Russian Collusion Dolls

"Russians make up a pretty disproportionate cross section of a lot of our assets. We see a lot of money pouring in from Russia."
— Donald Trump Jr. at a real estate conference in 2008

"We don't rely on American banks. We have all the funding we need out of Russia."
— Eric Trump

Rex Tillerson, the former chief executive of ExxonMobil from 2006 to 2016, and the 69th United States Secretary of State, **signed deals with the state-owned Russian oil company, Rosneft**, that was estimated at $500 billion. But in March 2014, under President Barack Obama, the U.S. imposed economic sanctions against Russia for its annexation of Crimea. The oil partnership was put on hold.

In April 2016, the leaked documents known as the **Panama Papers** outlined a **global system of tax evasion and implicated many government officials around the world**. The leak allowed $2 billion worth of offshore accounts to be traced back to Putin and his inner circle, including the trading of Rosneft shares.

Putin has blamed the U.S. for the leaks and, additionally, has blamed Hillary Clinton for inciting riots in Russia when she was the acting U.S. Secretary of State from 2009 to 2013. U.S. intelligence agencies detail in the report, "Assessing Russian Activities and Intentions in Recent US Elections: The Analytic Process and Cyber Incident Attribution." (also known as the Russia Hack Papers) how Putin wanted to undermine the 2016 U.S. elections.

During the Presidential debates, **Trump publicly encouraged Russia to hack Hillary Clinton's e-mail servers**. During his campaign, Trump made lifting the economic sanctions against Russia and improved relations with the foreign power a proposed element of his foreign policy.

"Russia, if you're listening, I hope you're able to find the 30,000 emails that are missing."
— Donald Trump, July 27, 2016

In December 2016, Jared Kushner met with **Michael Flynn and Sergey Gorkov**, the chairman of the Russian state-owned Vnesheconombank (VEB). Kushner's family's real estate holdings were having financial difficulties at the time.

Russian President Vladimir Putin appointed Gorkov to his job. Before that, he graduated in 1994 from the Russian Academy of Federal Counterintelligence Security Service, which trains people to work in Russia's intelligence and security forces.

On January 10, 2017, Buzzfeed released a **dossier that detailed kompromat (compromising or blackmail material) collected on Donald Trump**. The dossier was initially funded in 2016 as opposition research by Republican donors who opposed his run for the Republican nomination for president. When Trump secured the nomination, the Republican donors pulled their money to complete the dossier. Democratic donors then provided the funds to complete the dossier.

Visit Buzzfeed here to read the full dossier: **https://goo.gl/c5yttV**

As the Trump administration vilifies the Fourth Estate and undermines the freedom of the press, which is guaranteed by the 1st Amendment of the U.S. Constitution, it is now more important than ever for Americans to stay informed.

Visit **FAIR (Fairness & Accuracy in Reporting)** at **fair.org** to learn more about ways to detect media bias.

On February 2, 2017, Kellyanne Conway, Counselor to the President of the United States, referred to a **"Bowling Green Massacre"** to defend Trump's travel ban on seven majority-Muslim countries. **No such event has occurred at Bowling Green.**

White House Press Secretary Sean Spicer held contentious daily press briefings with the media before resigning on **July 21, 2017.**

Make SNL Great Again!

(Starring: Alec Baldwin, Melissa McCarthy, and Kate McKinnon)

"Get rid of [EPA] in almost every form. We are going to have little tidbits left but we are going to take a tremendous amount out."
— Donald Trump, March 2016

Since 1970, the Environmental Protection Agency has protected the air quality, waterways, food sources, and endangered species of America. **Scott Pruitt, Trump's pick as the 14th Administrator of the EPA**, previously served as head of the Republican Attorneys General Association, an organization that has accepted funds from the oil industry. The biggest donations this year came from oil conglomerate Koch Industries and Murray Energy, a leading coal mining company.

"Over the past five years, Pruitt has used his position as Oklahoma's top prosecutor to sue the EPA in a series of attempts to deny Americans the benefits of reducing mercury, arsenic, and other toxins from the air we breathe; cutting smog that can cause asthma attacks; and protecting our wetlands and streams."
— Rhea Suh, president of the Natural Resources Defense Council

Animals Protected Under The EPA

Animals Protected Under The EPA

"Should we tell him that's not an elected official?"

On January 28, 2017, Trump had a heated call with **Australian Prime Minister Malcolm Turnbull** over accepting refugees as part of their immigration policy. Vice President Mike Pence was sent to Australia in April to smooth over relations.

Since 1951, the U.S. and Australia have been bound by the Australia, New Zealand, United States Security Treaty (ANZUS or ANZUS Treaty) to co-operate in military matters. On trade matters, the Australia–United States Free Trade Agreement (AUSFTA) has been in effect since 2004.

According to a 2017 Lowy Institute Poll, **60% of Australians say Trump has caused them to have an unfavorable opinion of the U.S.**

Not like the brazen giant of Greek fame,
With conquering limbs astride from land to land;
Here at our sea-washed, sunset gates shall stand
A mighty woman with a torch, whose flame
Is the imprisoned lightning, and her name
MOTHER OF EXILES. From her beacon-hand
Glows world-wide welcome; her mild eyes command
The air-bridged harbor that twin cities frame.

"Keep, ancient lands, your storied pomp!" cries she
With silent lips. "Give me your tired, your poor,
Your huddled masses yearning to breathe free,
The wretched refuse of your teeming shore.
Send these, the homeless, tempest-tost to me,
I lift my lamp beside the golden door!"

"The New Colossus" by Emma Lazarus, 1883
Full inscription on the base of the Statue of Liberty

Democratic Governor of California Jerry Brown endorsed a **legal challenge to Trump's threats to pull federal funding from "sanctuary cities,"** or cities that limit cooperation with federal government and immigration authorities' attempts to enforce immigration law.

"California is in many ways out of control."
— Donald Trump, February 2017

"You don't want to mess with California."
— Jerry Brown (D-CA), March 2017

Upon his resignation from the White House in 1974, **President Richard Nixon** famously gave journalists double victory signs.

While **John McCain (R-AZ)**, left, dramatically voted against the "skinny repeal" (a partial repeal) of the Affordable Care Act on July 27, 2017, senators **Lisa Murkowski (R-AK)**, center, and **Susan Collins (R-ME)**, right, had long expressed their opposition to any repeal of the ACA and voted "no" on both repealing the ACA without a replacement on July 26, 2017 and to the skinny repeal the next day. A fourth senator, **Shelley Moore Capito (R-WV)**, also voted against repealing the ACA without replacement, but voted "yes" to the skinny repeal.

According to the *Washington Post*, a complete repeal of the ACA would have left 22 million Americans without health insurance, while the skinny repeal would have left 16 million uninsured.

Since January 20, 2017, the current administration has undergone a number of roster changes in addition to the departure of Steve Bannon.

Sean Spicer, Former White House Press Secretary (right)
in office from January 20, 2017 — July 21, 2017

Reinhold Richard "Reince" Priebus, Former White House Chief of Staff (left)
in office from January 20, 2017 — July 31, 2017

Anthony "The Mooch" Scaramucci, Former White House Director of Communications (center)
in office from July 21, 2017 — July 31, 2017

In the early 2000s, **Trump's casinos owed $30 million in taxes to the state of New Jersey**. After Chris Christie took office as Governor in 2010, the debt was reduced to $5 million. In April 2017, Christie vetoed a bill that would have required Donald Trump to release his tax returns in New Jersey to run for re-election.

Since being sworn into office, President Trump has engaged in brinkmanship with **Kim Jong-Un, Chairman of the Workers' Party of Korea and Supreme Leader of the Democratic People's Republic of Korea**, fuelled by reports of North Korea's growing intercontinental ballistic missile capabilities.

"North Korea best not make anymore threats to the United States [...] They will be met with fire, fury and frankly, power the likes of which this world has never seen before."
— Donald Trump, August 2017

"I will surely and definitely tame the mentally deranged U.S. dotard with fire."
— Chairman Kim Jong-Un, September 2017

This coloring book is a work of satire and is intended to inspire and entertain. The views expressed, and the illustrations contained herein are not affiliated, authorized, endorsed, or otherwise associated with any of the persons, businesses, organizations, governments mentioned herein, or any of its subsidiaries or affiliates. Unless otherwise noted, the views and opinions expressed herein are those of the creators.

Proceeds from the sale of this coloring book shall be donated to certain charities and organizations. A full list can be found on our Facebook page at **@AlternativeFactsColoringBook** or by emailing the creators at *alternativefactscoloringbook@gmail.com*. Such donations are made on the part of the creators, and have not been authorized, endorsed, or otherwise approved by any of the persons, businesses, organizations, governments mentioned herein.